BUILDING A HOUSE

BUILDING A HOUSE

KEN ROBBINS

FOUR WINDS PRESS
New York

ALSO BY KEN ROBBINS

Tools
Trucks of Every Sort

ACKNOWLEDGEMENTS

I would like to thank architects Gene Futterman and
Ernest Schieferstein, whose beautiful design became a
reality as I watched; Mr. and Mrs. Richard Fishbein, who
graciously allowed me to photograph a very private thing—
their home; Ed Johann, a superb craftsman who has been
more than generous with his time and special knowledge
of building; and Doug Kuntz, who took the photographs
that appear on page 45. Special thanks are also due to
Andy Moore and all of the workmen who, together, gave
this book its subject.

KEN ROBBINS

10 9 8 7 6 5 4 3 2 1

The text of this book is set in 11 pt. Primer.
The illustrations are black-and-white photographs.

Library of Congress Cataloging in Publication Data
Robbins, Ken.   Building a house.
Summary: Describes, step-by-step, how a house
is built from the architectural design through
the final installation of fixtures and fittings.
1. House construction—Juvenile literature.
[1. House construction] I. Title.
TH4811.5.R6   1984   690'.837   83-16513
ISBN 0-590-07887-9

REMEMBERING JOE,
who built houses.

This house belongs to the Fishbein family. It took almost a year and a half to build from the first planning stages to the day the furniture was moved in. More than 60 people worked on it. Some worked for months and others worked for less than a day. All together more than 10,000 hours of work went into building this house.

The wood from over 200 trees went into the construction, as well as 900 square feet of glass, 300 pounds of nails, 6,000 square feet of plasterboard, 2,500 square feet of tile, 35 tons of concrete, a ton of brick, and 35 gallons of paint.

The house is bigger and more expensive than most. But almost all houses are built in much the same way. What is important is that a house be built by skilled professional workers who care about their craft.

The process began when the Fishbeins went to see an architect, Gene Futterman (*upper right*), and asked him to design a house for them. The Fishbeins had seen several of the houses that Gene had designed, and they liked them. They already owned a piece of land, and they wanted to build a large, comfortable vacation house to use in the summer and on weekends. They wanted a bedroom and bathroom for themselves, another bedroom and bathroom for their daughter, Melissa, a bedroom for guests, a small den or music room, a living room, a dining area, and a kitchen. Since the house was to be a second home, they did not want a basement for storage or a garage.

Gene Futterman asked the Fishbeins about their hobbies, and how they liked to spend their time. He also asked them approximately how much money they wanted to spend on their house. Then he went to see the land the Fishbeins owned and made sketches to help him decide which way the house should face, and how the various rooms should be arranged. When he had all the information he needed, he and his associate, Ernie Schieferstein (*lower right*), began to create the design.

They showed the Fishbeins some drawings, as well as a model of the house that Ernie had built. This was the first time the Fishbeins could see what their house would look like. They studied the drawings and the model very carefully, and suggested some changes, which the architects made. Then Gene and Ernie made more than two dozen complete and accurate drawings, or plans, of every detail of the house.

Every person who worked on the house got his information from the plans that Gene and Ernie made. These plans show how the house will look from each side.

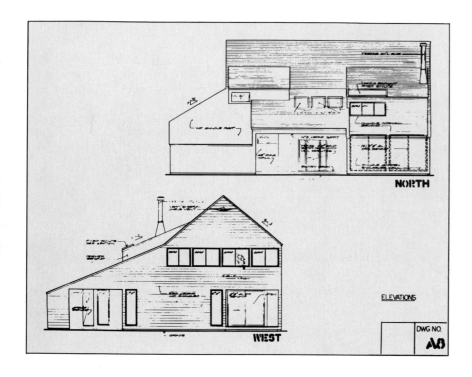

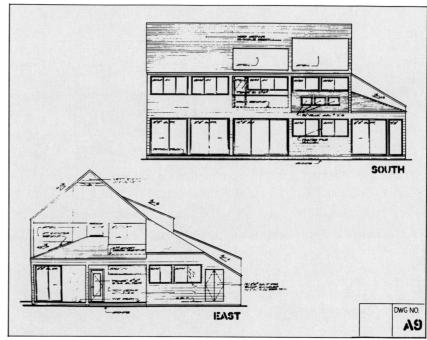

THE GENERAL CONTRACTOR

Andy Moore was the general contractor for the Fishbeins' house. He had already built several houses that Gene Futterman had designed. He had a reputation as a careful, intelligent, "quality" builder. Using the plans, he decided exactly what materials would be needed to build the house and approximately how much they would cost. The price of building materials can change dramatically from month to month. He consulted with the many subcontractors who work with him—carpenters, plumbers, electricians, and others. They told him how much they would charge to do their jobs. Then he calculated a price for his own time, labor, and risks, added it all up, and submitted it in the form of a bid—a formal offer to build the house for a specific price—to Gene Futterman. Gene presented Andy's bid to the Fishbeins, and when everyone was in agreement, a contract was signed and Andy Moore became the official general contractor of the house.

The general contractor has to know a great deal about all the work that goes into building a house. Though he will do little or none of the actual labor himself, he is responsible for all of it. Mostly, his job is to worry and make sure everything runs smoothly. In signing a contract, he promises to complete a specific house, built in a specific way, of specific materials, by a specific time, and for a specific price. If the quality of any of the work is poor, the contractor's reputation will suffer. So he worries about quality, about legal restrictions, late deliveries and delays, about bad weather, bad materials, and bad luck.

Most of the jobs involved in building a house are interdependent. Very often one job cannot be started until another has been completed. An electrician, for instance, cannot wait for a slow carpenter to finish his job—not if he wants to earn a living. He will go on to other jobs, and may not be available again. So careful scheduling is a necessity, and the general contractor worries about that.

THE SUPERVISOR

Since Andy often builds more than one house at a time, he hired a supervisor to oversee the building of the Fishbein house for him. A supervisor checks all work, gives advice to the workmen, and informs the general contractor of any problems.

THE SURVEYOR

Although the architect had indicated on a map the precise spot where the house was to be built, it was the surveyor's job to find and mark that spot on the land itself. He measured the correct distance from the edge of the Fishbeins' property with a special kind of telescope called a transit, and marked the corners of the house by driving wooden stakes in the ground.

THE EXCAVATION

Most wooden houses are not built directly on the ground. If they were, moisture in the earth would seep into the wood and cause it to rot. Instead, a concrete foundation, which often forms the basement of the house, is set in a hole in the ground and the house is built on top of it. The hole is called an excavation. Since the Fishbeins' house did not have a basement, but only a shallow area called a crawl space, the hole did not have to be very deep—five feet deep was enough. The excavation was dug in a few hours by one man operating a bulldozer.

THE FOUNDATION

The foundation was built on top of pads of concrete called footings. Wide and flat, they lie at the bottom of the excavation and keep the house from sinking into the moist ground.

At the bottom of the excavation, strings had been carefully stretched out to show the actual shape of the foundation. The masons, using the strings as guides, dug a shallow trench. Then they lined the sides of the trench with boards to make molds.

The cement trucks arrived and the workmen began pouring cement into the molds. The cement was dry the next day and the boards were removed. What remained was a hard, smooth, flat surface called a footing (*lower left*), on which the foundation of the house could be built.

Several days later the masons returned with a truck full of flat, wooden forms. They laid the forms around the inside and outside edges of the footings. Then they stood them up and locked them together, making a hollow wall.

The cement trucks came again. Workmen set up special chutes so the wet cement could be poured into the hollow spaces between the forms, filling them to just the right height.

When the concrete was hard and dry, the wooden forms were removed. What remained was the foundation—solid as a rock.

The walls of the foundation were coated with tar to keep moisture from seeping into the walls.

When the septic system was in place, the workmen used a bulldozer to push back over the foundation some of the earth that had been removed for the excavation. This is called backfilling. When it was done, the outside wall of the foundation could not be seen.

THE DECK

One morning a truck from the lumberyard delivered a stack of long, heavy boards. It was time for Ed Johann, the chief carpenter, and his assistants to begin work on the house.

Ed and his assistants worked with hammers, nails, tape measures, hand saws, and electric saws. Since there was no place to plug things in, they used a gasoline-powered generator to power the electric saws and tools *(lower right)*.

The carpenters first put a line of boards all along the top of the foundation. Then they fastened them with bolts that stick up out of the concrete foundation. These boards are called the sill, and they connect the entire house to the foundation.

Then longer, heavier boards called joists were cut to size and nailed in place from one side of the foundation to the other. In places they rest on pillars of concrete called piers. The piers keep the boards from sagging in the middle.

Finally, sheets of plywood were nailed to the joists, covering the open foundation and making what is called the deck, or the first floor, of the house.

FRAMING

The frame of a house is made of boards of different sizes and lengths. They hold the house up and give it its shape.

The vertical boards that form the walls are called studs *(lower left)*.

The sloping boards that support
the roof are called rafters *(right)*.
The horizontal boards are called
beams or joists *(below)*.

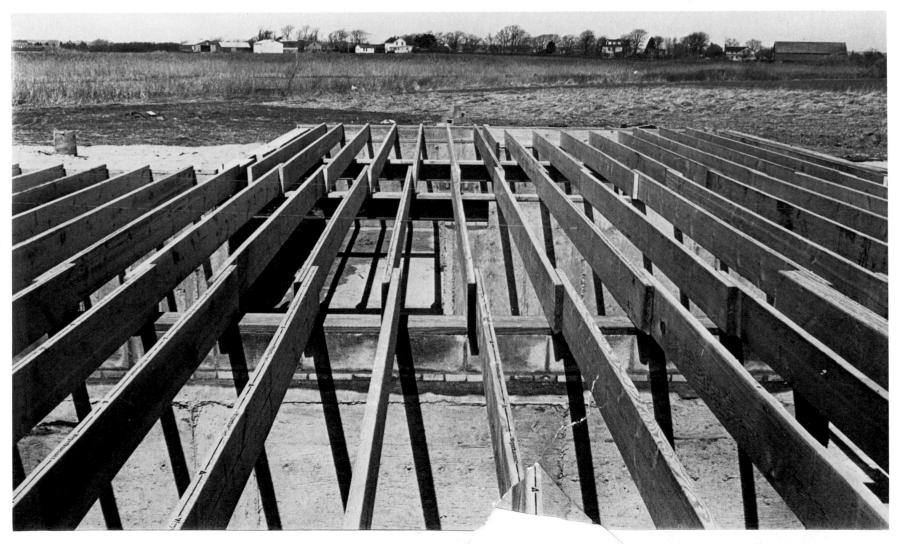

After cutting the boards to the right sizes, the carpenters nailed together an outside wall of the house, then stood it up in its proper place. Every board was cut exactly as shown in the architect's plans.

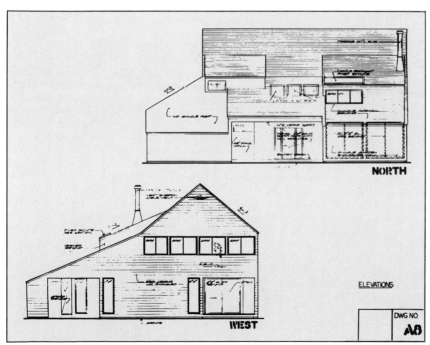

NORTH

ELEVATIONS

WEST

DWG NO. A8

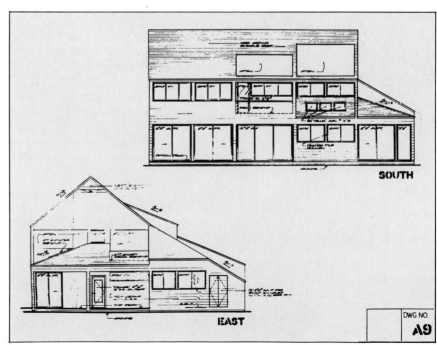

SOUTH

EAST

DWG NO. A9

As each section of the frame was added, more and
more of the size and shape of the house could be seen.

When the frame of the house is completed, it is a tradition in the United States and in many parts of the world to celebrate by nailing a small tree to the top of the roof. This is called topping out, and is usually the occasion for a party.

SHEATHING

When the framing was completed, the carpenters began enclosing the house by nailing sheets of plywood to the outside of the frame. Openings were left for the windows and doors. This process is called sheathing, and it not only closes the house in, but makes the frame much stronger.

Each part of the frame is firmly connected to all the other parts of the frame.

ROOFING

After the sides of the house were closed in with sheathing, the carpenters began nailing strips of wood, which are called lath, across the rafters of the roof.

Then bundles of flat pieces of cedar wood called shingles were hauled up onto the roof. Cedar shingles make especially good roofs because cedar does not easily rot. One by one the shingles were nailed to the lath in an overlapping pattern.

SIDING

Black tar paper was stapled to the plywood sheathing on the sides of the house. The tar paper helps to keep moisture out of the house. Shingles were nailed in place on top of the tar paper.

WINDOWS

While the carpenters were nailing up the shingles, three men from the glass company installed the glass doors and windows. First, they assembled the metal frames for the large sliding glass doors.

Then, they carefully placed the frames in the openings left by the carpenters.

Finally, they put the glass doors in place and fitted them with locks.

The frames for the windows had been put together at the factory, and were installed in the same way as the glass doors.

By the time the glaziers finished installing the glass doors and windows, the roof was also complete, and the carpenters had hung the wooden front door. The house was now "closed in." The inside was protected from wind and rain and the electrician and the plumber could begin their work.

ELECTRICITY

It is the electrician's job to run wires through the walls of the house. The wires connect every electrical switch and outlet to the place in the crawl space where the power company's electrical supply cable enters the house.

Boxes for switches, outlets, and light fixtures were nailed to the studs.

Then holes were drilled through the floors and studs, and long lengths of wire were threaded through the holes.

Later, all the boxes were connected to the right wires and all the wires were connected to the supply cable. It was now possible to have power and light in the house.

THE PLUMBER

The plumber installs all the pipes that bring water to the many different faucets in the house, and that carry waste from all the drains to the septic system. The fresh water is carried through copper pipes called supply lines. The wastes are carried through thicker, white plastic pipes called waste lines (*below*).

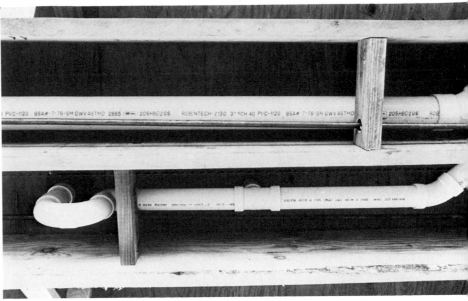

Both kinds of pipe run under the floors and inside the walls of the house. The plumber's first job was to drill or cut the holes through which the pipes would run. When the pipes were in place, sections of the waste lines were joined with glue. The metal supply lines were heated with a blow torch and sealed together with a combination of melted lead and tin called solder. Joining pipes this way is called sweating.

As the plumber and the electrician were finishing their work, the heating contractor cut vent holes in the floors of each room—two holes in the smaller rooms, more in larger ones.

Long, rectangular tubes called ducts were then placed under the floor and inside the walls so that each vent hole connected to a central spot in the crawl space.

Finally, all the ducts were connected to an electric furnace. In the winter this furnace will produce heat, and an electric fan will blow hot air from the furnace through the ducts to every room in the house.

INSULATION

All the walls and ceilings were lined with fiberglass insulation. This keeps the heat inside the house.

Fiberglass insulation comes in long, rolled up strips called bats. The strips were cut to the right length and stapled in place between all the studs and rafters.

SHEETROCK

Once the wiring, plumbing, and insulation were in place, the inside walls and ceilings were covered with Sheetrock. Sheetrock is a sheet of plaster sandwiched between two sheets of heavy paper.

Each piece of Sheetrock was carefully measured to fit in its proper place. Although it is quite heavy, Sheetrock is easily cut with a knife.

The pieces were nailed in place with special nails that will not easily pull out. Holes were cut for all the light fixtures, switches, and electrical outlets.

SPACKLING

The spackler fills in all the cracks and smooths out all the joints and corners between the pieces of Sheetrock.

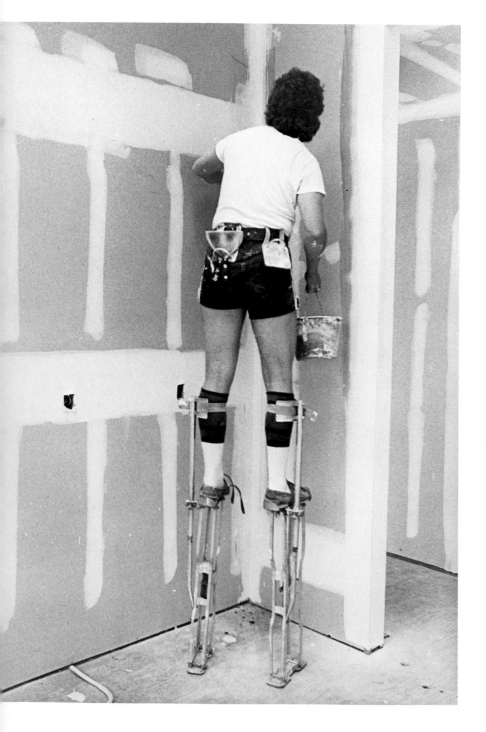

Working with wet plaster called joint compound, the spackler smeared just the right amount onto each joint, and pressed a long strip of paper tape over that. Then with a tool called a trowel, he smoothed down the plaster and pressed the tape over the joint.

Using stilts and ladders to reach the ceilings and the upper parts of the walls, he made his way around the entire house. By the time he had finished, the first joints were dry, and it was time to go back over everything with a second, and then a third coat of compound. With each coat the joints got smoother and smoother until finally they could no longer be seen at all.

FLOORING

The Fishbeins wanted slate tiles on their floors. The tilers put a mixture of sand and cement, called mud, on top of the plywood deck. Then they smoothed it out with long, flat trowels and boards so that it became perfectly level and flat.

When the mud was dry and hard they laid the slate tiles in place and filled the gaps between them with a special cement called grout.

PAINTING

After carefully covering all the tile floors to protect them from drips and spills, the painter put two coats of white paint on all the walls and ceilings. He used a roller for the flat areas, and a brush to paint into the corners and around windows.

FIXTURES AND FITTINGS

The house was nearly completed, but a number of jobs remained to be done. While the painter was working, the electrician came back to install the light fixtures. Cabinetmakers delivered and installed the kitchen counters, cabinets, and washstands. The plumber came back to install the toilets, sinks, and showers, as well as appliances such as the dishwasher and laundry machines.

Doors and door knobs for the inside of the house were installed.

FINAL TOUCHES

Outside, gravel for the driveway was spread and grass was planted. The furniture was delivered, and the Fishbeins moved in. The house, which had taken so long to build, suddenly became a home.